THE SECOND FOLK DANCE BOOK

COMPILED BY

C. WARD CRAMPTON

DIRECTOR OF PHYSICAL TRAINING, NEW YORK CITY

AUTHOR OF "THE FOLK DANCE BOOK"

New York

A. S. BARNES AND COMPANY

1922

INTRODUCTION.

"The Folk Dance Book," published seven years ago, has been adopted generally throughout the United States. It has fulfilled its purpose in presenting a clear, concise description of the most useful and attractive folk dances appropriate for schools and playgrounds.

In response to a wide-spread demand for more dances, this "Second Folk Dance Book" is published. During the last seven years many new forms of folk plays and dances have been collected and tested. The best have been selected and are included in this collection.

Folk Dances have ceased to be a fad. They are now used in connection with formal physical training as a delightful means of obtaining hygienic, educational and recreative results of normal exercise.

Acknowledgment is made to Miss Annie Collan for the original arrangement of many Finnish dances; to Miss Maude Edmunds and Miss Ellen Hope Wilson for the collection and trial of several dances; and to Miss Emily O'Keefe, Inspector of Athletics for Girls, for assembling the material.

THE EDITOR.

April, 1916.

LIST OF DANCES.

Arranged in order of difficulty.

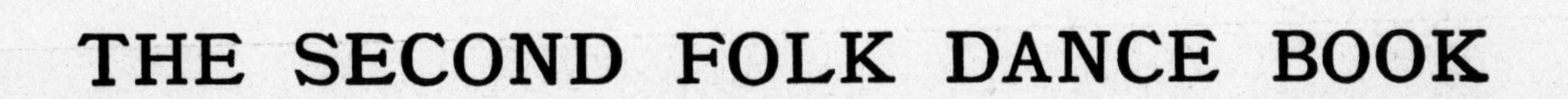

THE SECOND FOLK DANCE BOOK

OUR LITTLE GIRLS.

Formation. In large circle facing centre (Fig. 1). Four girls on inside of circle.

Measures 1–16. Large circle walk thirty-two steps to left, swinging arms. Four girls on inside walk thirty-two steps in opposite direction to outside circle. On seventeenth step inside girls each take a partner from the large circle and walk with her hand in hand.

Measures 1–8. Large circle skip sixteen steps continuing to left. Couples inside join both hands and skip sixteen steps, turning in place.

Measures 9–16. All walk sixteen steps. Large circle continuing to left, inside couples hand in hand in opposite direction.

Repeat all.

Fig. 1. In large circle facing centre.

OUR LITTLE GIRLS.

For boomferalla, boomferalla,
Boomferalla la,
For boomferalla la,
For boomferalla la.
And if thou wilt be
A partner to me,
Then take my hand in dancing,
And sing so merrily.

SEVEN PRETTY GIRLS IN A RING.

Formation. Large circle, all hands joined, seven or more girls in small circle on inside of large circle—hands joined.

Measures 1–8. Outside circle moves to left with twenty-four light running steps. Inside circle moves to right with twenty-four steps.

Measures 1–8. Outside circle continues as above. Inside circle clap hands and face outward, join hands again and continue on in same direction.

Measures 1–8. Girls of inside circle choose a partner from outside circle and bring her into the circle. Nod alternately right and left to partner, extend right hand to partner and shake hands. Outside circle stands still during this verse.

Measures 1–8. Inside couples clap hands, hook right arms with partner and turn her—twelve running steps; clap hands, change to left arms and turn in opposite direction twelve steps. Outside circle runs to left twenty-four steps.

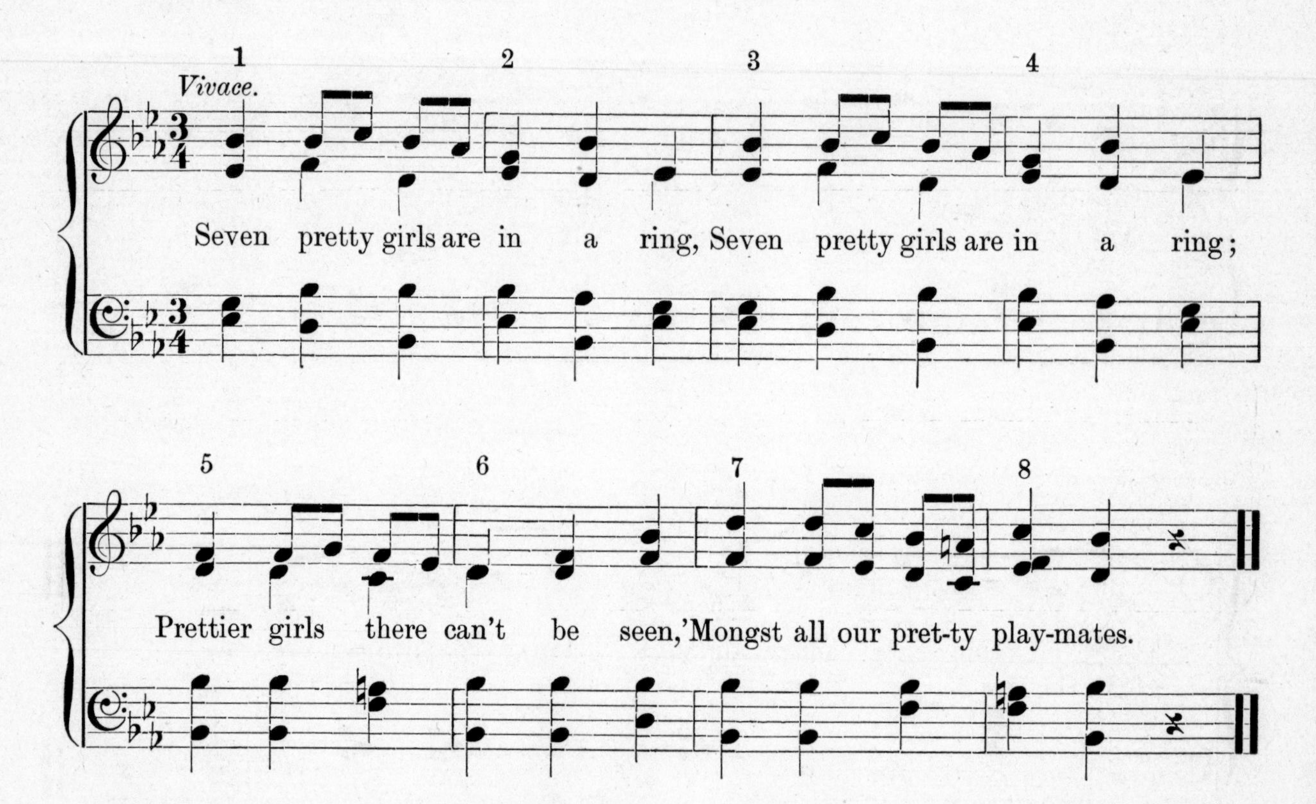

Girls! turn, oh, turn yourselves about,
Girls! turn, oh, turn yourselves about;
Come, choose ye each a partner out,
Tra la la la la la la.

Now am I thine, if thou art mine,
Now am I thine, if thou art mine;
Take then the hand I give as sign
That I am now thy partner.

Now we are happy all the day,
Now we are happy all the day,
So let us sing and dance and play,
Tra la la la la la la.

GREETING AND MEETING.

Formation. Double circle, partners facing. (See Fig. 6.)
Measures 1–2. Inside partners make deep curtsey.
Measures 3–4. Outside partners make deep curtsey.
Measures 5–6. Inside partners hold out both hands to their partners.
Measures 7–8. Outside partners take their partner's offered hands.
Measures 1–8. All skip around circle, inside hands joined, outside hands on hips.
Repeat as often as desired.

OUT RODE A RIDER.

Formation. Single circle, hands joined. (See Fig 1.) A horse and rider are inside of the circle; the rider drives the horse with light rein passed over his shoulders and under his arm pits.

Step. Gallop step—two to each measure.

Measures 1–14. Outside circle gallops to left. Rider on inside drives his horse in opposite direction. On words "Ride Away," the rider holds his horse with his left hand and tries to catch a boy from the outside circle with his right hand. The boy caught becomes the horse while the horse becomes the driver, and the last driver goes back into the ring. The game is then repeated.

NEST MAKING.

Formation. In large double circle, partners facing. (See Fig. 6.)

Measure 1. Begin left, four walking steps backward, clap hands on first step.

Measure 2. Begin left, four walking steps forward, clap hands on first step.

Measures 3–4. Take partner's both hands, and turn partner, swinging around to left, eight light running steps.

Measures 1–4. Repeat above.

Measures 5–8. Both large circles take hands and with sixteen running steps each circle moves to left.

Measures 5–8. Circles return to right with sixteen running steps.

Measure 1. Imitate motion of chopping, using two counts, and then motion of planing, using two counts.

Measure 2. Clap both hands together, clap partner's right. Clap both hands together, clap partner's left.

Measures 3–4. Same as measures 3–4 above.

Measures 1–4. Repeat measures 1–4, imitating chopping and planing again.

Measures 5–8. Same as measures 5–8 above.

Measure 1. Simple curtsey to partner, stepping back on left foot.

Measure 2. Pivot to left on toes and curtsey to rear.

Measures 3–4. Same as measures 3–4 above.

Measures 1–4. Repeat curtsey.

Measures 5–8. Same as 5–8 above.

MASKROSOR.

Formation. In sets of two couples facing centre. Inside hands joined with partner—outside hand on hip.

Measures 1–2. Two schottische steps across to opposite side—one couple passes through centre and the other separates and passes on outside.

Measures 3–4. Two schottische steps backward into place. The couple that separated crossing over passes through centre going back.

Measures 5–6. Ladies give right hand to opposite lady and with two schottische steps cross to opposite gentlemen.

Measures 7–8. Ladies give left hand to opposite gentlemen and couple turns once around with two schottische steps.

Measures 9–10. Ladies give right hand to opposite ladies and return to own partner with two schottische steps.

Measures 11–12. Take partner's both hands and with arms out at sides, turn partners, four hops.

Measures 1–4. All join hands in circle and move to left with four schottische steps.

Measures 5–8. Face about—all grasp left hands in centre and return to place with four schottische steps.

Measures 9–10. In place with inside hand joined with partner's—balance to outside—balance in inside.

Measures 11–12. Turn partners with four hops.

PEER SPELMAN.

Formation. Large single circle, all facing center, hands grasped.
Measure 1. Step left foot to left, bring right foot up to it.
Measures 2–8. Repeat measure 1.
Measure 9. Step on left, swing right in front and repeat to right.
Measure 10. Repeat measure 9.
Measure 11. Curtsey: Boys bring heels together and bow. Girls put right toe behind left heel and make a bobbing curtsey.

TO-DAY'S THE FIRST OF MAY.

Formation. In double circle, couples facing forward, circle moving from right to left. (Fig. 2.)

Inside hands joined, outside hands on hips.

Measures 1–8. Begin inside foot and turn away from partner on first step. Eight polka steps around circle, turning away from and toward partners; finish facing partners in double circle.

Measures 9–10. Shake hands with partners three times.

Measures 11–16. Clap hands once; face to the right and skip half around circle to meet partner.

Repeat dance from beginning.

New partners may be secured by passing your own partner in the skip around, measures 11–16, and taking the one next to her for the repeat of the dance.

FIG. 2. Double circle, couples facing forward.

TO-DAY'S THE FIRST OF MAY.

GUSTAF'S SKOAL.

Formation. In sets of four couples facing centre, (Fig. 3) two head couples standing opposite and two side couples standing opposite.

Measures 1–2. Head couples walk three steps forward towards centre and make a bobbing bow to opposite couple.

Measures 3–4. Same couples—four steps backward to place.

Measures 5–8. Side couples same.

Measures 1–4. Head couples repeat.

Measures 5–8. Side couples repeat.

Measures 9–12. Side couples make arch with inside hands grasped and held high. Head couples skip forward toward centre, separate and take hands of opposite, then skip through arch and around to place, meeting own partner.

Measures 13–16. All clap hands once, take both hands of partner and skip in place turning to the right, pulling away from each other.

Measures 9–16. Repeat—head couples holding arch, side couples skipping around.

Repeat from beginning.

Fig. 3. Four couples facing centre.

GUSTAF'S SKOAL.

SWISS MAY DANCE.

Formation. Double Circle. Partners face forward. (See Fig. 2, page 16.) Inside hands joined, outside holding skirts.

Measures 1–3. Nine running steps forward.

Measure 4. Partners face each other and curtsey, holding skirts with both hands.

Measures 5–7. Face about and run nine steps to position.

Measure 8. Partners face each other and curtsey.

Measure 9. Join right hands and take three running steps forward, changing places with partner.

Measure 10. Face partner and curtsey.

Measures 11–12. Repeat 9–10, crossing with left hands joined.

Measures 13–14. Join right hands. Outside partner run in place, six steps. Inside partner turn under raised arm of partner with six running steps.

Measure 15. Inside partner run in place, three steps. Outside partner run forward three steps to next partner.

Measure 16. All bow as above.

Repeat from beginning.

SWISS MAY DANCE.

RITSCH, RATSCH.

Formation. Sets of four each facing centre, hands on hips.
Measure 1. Clap hands twice and place hands on hips.
Measure 2. Hop right and place left foot forward, toe raised.
Measure 3. Change feet, placing right foot in front.
Measure 4. Change again, placing left foot in front.
Measures 5–8. Repeat 1–4.
Measures 9–10. Bend trunk forward and raise.
Measures 11–12. Bend knees and stretch.
Measures 13–14. Bend trunk and raise.
Measures 15–16. Bend knees and stretch.
Measures 17–24. Join hands in small circle and skip sixteen steps moving to left.

RITSCH, RATSCH.

KNYTNAPSPOLSKA.

Formation. In couples, facing partners; both hands joined and pulling back away from partners.

Step. The Polska step is executed thus: Polska step.—Begin left, slide twice to left (slide, close, slide) and leap on to right foot across in front of left foot. This step is also done beginning right foot and leaping on to left.

Measures 1–3. Begin left, three polska steps to left.

Measure 4. Stamp left, stamp right, stamp left.

Measures 1–3. Three polska steps to right.

Measure 4. Stamp right, stamp left, stamp right.

Measure 5. Both jump and land on both feet, turning so that right elbow points towards partner. Hands on hips.

Measure 6. Jump again, facing so that left elbow points towards partner.

Measure 7. Repeat measure 5, this time shake clenched fist at partner.

Measure 8. Repeat measure 6 and shake left fist at partner.

Measures 5–8. Join hands with partner and twist in place, pivoting on right foot. End with a stamp of left foot on last count.

SANDAL POLKA.

Formation. Double circle, partners facing line of direction. (See Fig. 2, page 16.) Inside hands joined, outside hands on hips.

Measure 1. Step sideways with left foot and close with right foot.

Measure 2. Repeat.

Measures 3–4. Both hands on hips. With four running steps make a half turn to the left to face in opposite direction.

Measures 1–2. Same as measures 1–2 above.

Measures 3–4. With half turn to the left face in line of direction with four running steps.

Measures 5–8. Inside hands joined and outside hands on hips. Skip sixteen steps around circle.

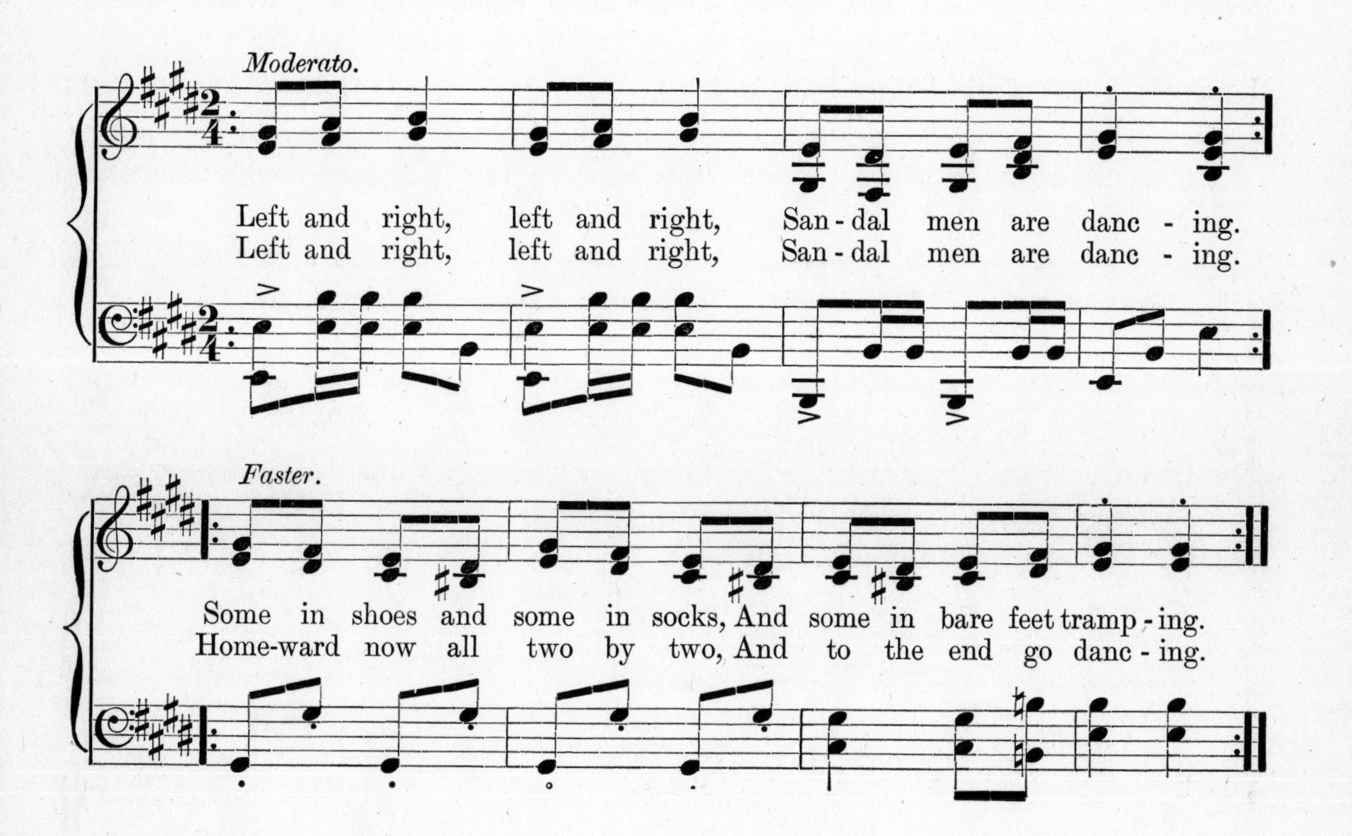

COME HAUL THE WATER.

Formation. Double circle, couples facing, both hands joined.

Measure 1. Man steps to side with left foot and brings right foot up to it. Lady does the same, beginning with right foot.

Measure 2. Repeat measure 1.

Measure 3. Man steps to side with right foot and brings left up to it. Lady does the same, beginning with left foot.

Measure 4. With heels together raise and lower heels slightly, keeping time to music.

Measures 5–8. Repeat measures 1–4.

Measures 9–10. Man drops grasp of lady's right hand. Man still holds lady's left hand in his right. Both turn once around to outside with two waltz steps.

Measure 11. With both hands grasped again, man steps left and brings right foot up to it. Lady does the same. beginning with right foot.

Measures 12–13. Repeat measure 11.

Measure 14. Man steps to side with right foot and brings left up to it. Lady does the same, beginning with left foot.

Measure 15. Man drops lady's right hand, and turns her under his arm. Lady makes turn to outside with one waltz step.

Measure 16. Lady curtsies, man bows.

COME HAUL THE WATER.

THE CRESTED HEN.

Formation. Circles of three, hands joined, number dancers 1–2–3. (Fig. 4.)

Step: Step-hop raising foot quickly from floor each time.

Measures 1–8. Dance eight steps starting with left foot and moving in circle to left.

Measure 1. Stamp with left foot.

Measures 2–8. Dance seven steps, starting with right foot and moving in circle to right. Finish in one line, 1 and 3 dropping hands. 2 standing in centre holding hands of 1 and 3. (Fig. 5.)

Measures 9–12. Number 1 dances four steps crossing in front of number 2, passing under arms of 2 and 3 and on to her own place. Number 2 dances four steps turning in place in same direction as number 1.

Measures 13–16. Number 3 dances four steps crossing in front of number 2, passing under the arms of 1 and 2 and on to her own place. Number 2 dances four steps turning in place in same direction as number 3.

Measures 8–12. Number 1 repeat.

Measures 13–16. Number 3 repeat.

Repeat from beginning.

Fig. 4. Circles of three.

THE CRESTED HEN.

FIG. 5. Finish in one line.

HANSEL AND GRETEL.

Formation. Double circle, facing partners. (Fig. 6.)
Measures 1–2. Step away from partner and curtsey. Return to position.
Measures 3–4. Take partner's both hands.
Measure 5. Point forward toe to side, point forward toe in back.
Measure 6. Polka step in line of direction.
Measures 7–8. Same as in measures 5–6, but in opposite direction.
Measures 9–16. All partners skip sixteen steps around circle with inside hands joined, outside hands on hips.
Measure 17. Stand still.
Measure 18. Stamp three times, right, left, right.
Measure 19. Stand still.
Measure 20. Clap three times. Take partner's both hands.
Measures 21–24. Same as measures 5–8.
Repeat dance. At measure 18, nod three times.
At measure 20, snap fingers three times.

Fig. 6. Double circle, facing partners.

HANSEL AND GRETEL DANCE.

CORNISH MAY DANCE.

Formation. Double circle facing forward. (See Fig. 2, page 16.) Inside hands joined, outside hands on hips.

Measures 1–8. Sixteen skip steps forward around circle. Finish, couples facing in sets of four.

Measure 9. Two skip steps forward to meet opposite couples of set.

Measure 10. Two skip steps backward to place.

Measures 11–12. Four skip steps forward, passing through to opposite side of set, one couple passing through centre, the other on outside of set, and all face centre again.

Measure 9. On repeat. Two skip steps to meet opposite couples again.

Measure 10. Two skip steps back to place.

Measures 11–12. Four skip steps forward and pass through back to place in reverse order of measures 11–12 as above. Form in circle of four, hands joined.

Measures 1–4. In circle to left. Skip eight steps, once around to place and drop hands.

Measure 5. Take partner's hand and dance two skip steps to opposite partners.

Measure 6. Two skip steps back to place.

Measures 7–8. Four skip steps passing through to opposite side of set.

All face forward around circle and repeat dance from beginning.

CORNISH MAY DANCE.

TREKARLSPOLSKA.

Formation. In three lines of three each, about four feet apart, the two end lines facing in towards centre of set and the middle line facing the line at one end. Each line has one gentleman and two ladies. Gentleman in centre joins hands with lady on either side and holds arms half bent. For convenience number the lines One at end, Two in the middle, and Three at the other end.

Step. Ostgota Step. Begin left foot, slide twice to left, (slide, close, slide) and step right foot across in front. Continue to left.

Measures 1–2. Salute. Lines One and Two, beginning left, take three running steps towards each other and stamp right foot forward on last count.

Measures 3–4. Same lines take three running steps back to place. The centre line on last count drop hands, jump facing about and catch up hands again.

Measures 5–6. Lines Two and Three, beginning left, take three running steps towards each other and stamp right foot forward on last count.

Measures 7–8. Same lines run three steps back to place, centre line facing about on last count.

The above is repeated after each figure.

Measures 1–2. Gentleman in line Two begins left foot, runs three steps forward and stamps right foot in front of lady at right end of line One.

Measures 3–4. Same gentleman stamps left foot, right foot, and at same time lady stamps left and right foot forward.

Measures 5–8. Gentleman places hands at lady's waist. Lady places hands on gentleman's shoulder. Gentleman turns partner with four Ostgota steps.

Measures 9–10. Same gentleman runs three steps to lady in diagonally opposite corner of set and stamps right foot forward.

Measures 11–12. Same gentleman stamps left, stamps right foot and at same time lady stamps right and left foot forward.

Measures 13–16. Gentleman turns partner with four Ostgota steps.

Measures 9–16. Same gentleman forms a ring with the two ladies with whom he has danced; the lady on the left of line Two forms a circle with the other lady and gentleman of line One, and the lady on the right of line Two forms a circle with the other lady and gentleman of line Three.

All dance four Ostgota steps in circle beginning left. At end all fall back into original lines.

Measures 1–8. Repeat salute described in measures 1–8.

Measures 1–16. Gentleman in line Two runs three steps forward and stamps to lady at left end of line One. Gentleman of line Two repeats his dance described in second 1–8 measures, but dances with ladies on left of line One and Three this time.

TREKARLSPOLSKA (continued).

Measures 9–16. Same gentleman forms circle with ladies with whom he has just danced, lady on right of line Two forms circle with other lady and gentleman of line One and lady on left of line Two forms circle with other lady and gentleman of line Three. All dance four Ostgota steps in circle.

Measures 1–8. Repeat salute.

Measures 1–16. Gentleman of line Two repeats dance described in first 1–8 measures, but dances with his own partners, first with lady on his right and then with lady on his left.

Measures 9–16. Each line form circle and dance four Ostgota steps.

Measures 1–8. Gentleman of line Two dances with gentleman of line One and threatens with his closed fist when stamping feet forward, other gentleman responding in like manner. Repeat with gentleman of line Three.

Measures 1–8. Gentlemen form ring in centre, ladies form ring outside of gentlemen and all dance four Ostgota steps in circle.

TREKARLSPOLSKA.

SKANSKA QUADRILLE.

Formation. In set, one couple on each side of four sides; two head couples, two side couples. (See Fig. 3.)

FIGURE 1. All in a circle.

Measures 1–8. Join hands, ladies facing centre, gentlemen facing outside. Gentlemen start right, ladies start left, sixteen walking steps around in a circle.

Measures 1–8. Return to place, sixteen brisk walking steps.

Measures 9–16. Turn partner in place with sixteen pivot steps; gentlemen place both hands at partner's waist, ladies both hands on partner's shoulders.

Measures 17–18. Head couples, beginning with outside foot, advance to centre with four walking steps.

Measures 19–20. Pivot on toes, turn to rear, and beginning with inside foot, return to place with four walking steps, accenting first step.

Measures 21–24. Side couples do the same. All this is called the "Push."

Measures 25–26. Head couples take four step-hops to the centre, meeting opposite head couples.

Measures 27–28. Four step-hops back to place.

Measures 29–32. Eight step-hops forward and pass through to the opposite side, quickly facing in towards centre again. Ladies passing on inside.

Measures 25–32. Head couples repeat, returning to place. All this (measures 25–32 and repeat) is called the "Balance."

Measures 17–24. Side couples starting and head couples following, repeat the "Push."

Measures 25–32. Side couples balance.

FIGURE 2. Maiden's Ring.

Measures 1–8. Ladies join hands in circle on inside of set, gentlemen in place clapping hands and beating time with right foot. Ladies walk sixteen steps to left in circle.

Measures 1–8. Ladies sixteen brisk steps to right in circle.

Measures 9–16. Turn partners in place sixteen pivot steps.

Measures 17–24. "Push," head couples leading, side couples following.

Measures 25–32. Head couples balance.

Measures 17–24. "Push," side couples leading, head couples following.

Measures 25–32. Side couples balance.

FIGURE 3. Youths' Ring.

Measures 1–8. Men join hands in circle on inside of set, facing outside. Walk sixteen steps around in circle beginning right foot, ladies clap hands and beat time with right foot.

STANSKA QUADRILLE (continued).

Measures 1–8. Men return to place with sixteen brisk walking steps.
Measures 9–10. Turn partner in place with sixteen pivot steps.
Measures 17–24. "Push," head couples leading, side couples following.
Measures 25–32. Head couples balance.
Measures 17–24. "Push," sides leading, and head couples following.
Measures 25–32. Head couples balance.

FIGURE 4. Each with his own.

Measures 1–2. Men step around inside of set and stand facing their partners. Lady dances backward away from partner four step-hops and man follows her.
Measures 3–4. Man dances backward to place four step-hops and lady follows.
Measures 5–6. Man dances four step-hops backward to the centre of set and lady follows.
Measures 7–8. Lady dances four step-hops backward to place and man follows.
Measures 9–16. Turn partner sixteen pivot steps.
Measures 17–24. "Push," head couples leading, side couples following.
Measures 25–32. Head couples balance.
Measures 17–24. "Push," side couples leading, head couples following.
Measures 25–32. Side couples balance.

FIGURE 5.

Measures 1–8. Repeat first figure.
Measures 9–16. Turn partner sixteen pivot steps.

STANSKA QUADRILLE (continued).

POLISH KRAKOVIAK.

Formation. In couples, partners facing.

Measure 1. All stamp right, stamp left, stamp right, and tap left heel against floor and swing left foot slightly forward.

Measure 2. Same as measure 1, beginning left foot.

Measure 3. Walk two steps to right, beginning right foot. This takes partners away from each other.

Measure 4. Repeat measure 1.

Measure 5. Repeat measure 2.

Measure 6. Repeat measure 1.

Measure 7. Walk two steps to left to original position opposite partner.

Measure 8. Repeat measure 2.

Measure 9–16. In waltz position, partners dance about room thus: Man hops on left foot, step right and hop right; hop right, step left and hop left and continue. Lady begins with right foot.

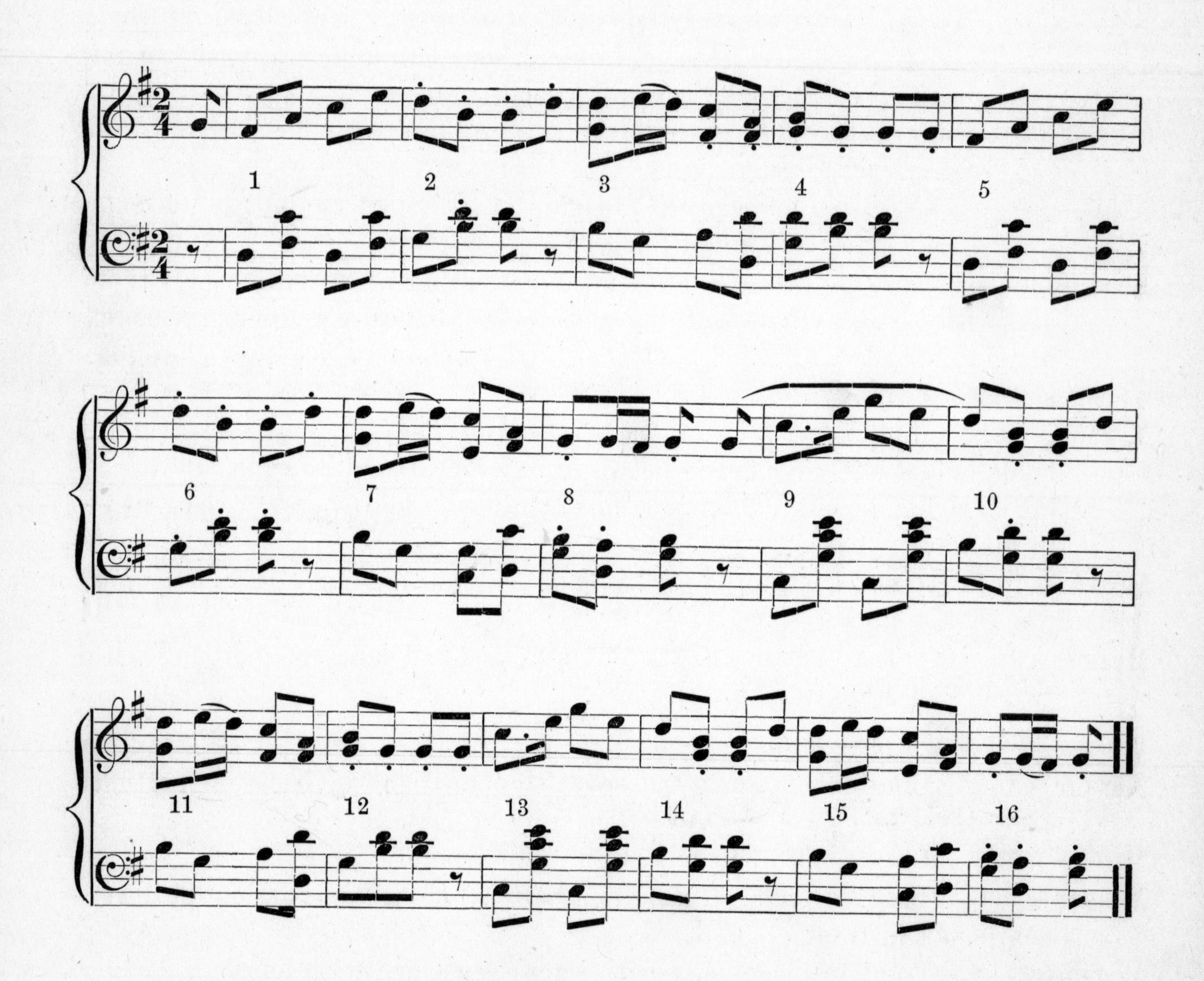

IRISH FOUR HAND JIG.

Formation. In sets of two couples facing centre. One couple the leading couple, and one the opposite couple.

All arms hang at sides unless otherwise indicated.

Seven-Step.
1. Spring and land lightly on both feet, right foot in advance.
2. Step right foot to side on ball of foot.
3. Step left foot across behind right.
4. Step right to right side.
5. Step left foot across behind right.

6 and 7. Repeat 4 and 5.

Point. To right.
1. Spring off floor and land on both feet, right foot across in front.
2. Hop on left and raise right in front.
3. Hop left and swing right behind and beat 1-2-3-4, i. e., right behind, left in front, and repeat, behind and in front.

To left. Start left foot in front. Raise left foot in front. In the beating, left foot is behind.

1-2-3-4 Step. 1-2. Hop on left foot and at the same time step forward with right.

3. Bring left foot up to right. Left toe at heel of right foot.

4. Step forward with right foot.

Lead around. Measures 1–6. Gentleman takes partner's left hand in his right and with his left elbow touching left elbow of opposite gentleman (hands hanging at side), all start right foot and lead around counter clockwise six 1-2-3-4 steps.

Measures 7–8. Hands over. Gentleman raises his right hand with which he holds lady's left, over lady's head, turning her around to right and turning to right himself. Change hands, gentleman taking lady's right hand in his left.

Measures 9–14. Lead back to place, this time gentlemen's right elbows touching. Six 1-2-3-4 steps.

Measures 15–16. Take partner's both hands crossed and dance once around with two 1-2-3-4 steps and stop in place.

Body. Seven-step and point.

Measures 1–2. Gentleman takes one seven-step to right in back of partner. Lady takes one seven-step to left in front of partner.

Measures 3–4. Gentlemen point with right, ladies point with left.

Measures 5–6. Both seven-step back to original place, lady passing in back, gentleman in front.

Measures 7–8. Point in place, lady with right, gentleman with left.

IRISH FOUR HAND JIG (continued).

Half right and left.

Measures 9–10. Take partner's hands crossed and dance around in place with two 1-2-3-4 steps.

Measures 11–12. Gentlemen exchange places, passing left arms to left arms with two 1-2-3-4 steps.

Measures 13–14. Ladies exchange places, passing right arms to right arms with two 1-2-3-4 steps.

Measures 15–16. All point in place with outside foot, gentleman left, lady right foot.

Measures 1–8. Seven step and point. Repeat measures 1–8 above.

Measures 9–16. Half right and left. Repeat measures 9–16 above.

FIGURE 1. Advance through centre.

Measures 1–2. Leading couples take hands and advance to centre. Two 1-2-3-4 steps.

Measures 3–4. Pass through centre of opposite couple and beyond. Two 1-2-3-4 steps.

Measures 5–6. Both face about turning towards each other, join hands again and advance to centre of opposite couple again. Two 1-2-3-4 steps.

Measures 7–8. Lady takes opposite gentleman's left hand in her left. Gentleman takes opposite lady's right hand in his right. All turn around once. Two 1-2-3-4 steps.

Measures 9–10. Leading couples join inside hands again and advance to their own place. Six 1-2-3-4 steps.

Measures 11–12. Both face about, turning in toward partners and advance to centre again. Two 1-2-3-4 steps.

Measures 13–14. Lady takes opposite gentleman's right hand in her right hand, and gentleman takes opposite lady's left hand in his left. All turn around once in place. Two 1-2-3-4 steps.

Measures 15–16. Head couples return to place with two 1-2-3-4 steps.

Measures 1–16. Opposite couples repeat figure.

Measures 1–16 and repeat. Repeat BODY of dance.

FIGURE 2. Centre meet.

Measures 1–2. Leading gentleman and opposite lady clasp hands and dance seven steps to gentleman's right.

Measures 3–4. Point. Gentleman with right, lady with left.

Measures 5–8. Drop hands. Gentleman makes quarter turn to the left and lady quarter turn to the right. Gentleman takes his own partner's left hand in his left, and lady takes her own partner's right in her right. All turn around once with four 1-2-3-4 steps.

IRISH FOUR HAND JIG (continued).

Measures 9–10. Leading gentlemen and opposite lady seven steps back to place.

Measures 11–12. Point. Lady with right, gentleman with left.

Measures 13–16. Drop hands. Take quarter turn, gentleman to right, lady to left. Gentleman takes own partner's right hand in his right, lady takes own partner's left in her left. All turn partners to place. Four 1-2-3-4 steps.

Measures 1–16. Leading lady and opposite gentleman repeat figure.

Measures 1–16 and repeat. Repeat Body.

Finish.

Measures 1–3. All join right hands in centre, and dance around with three 1-2-3-4 steps.

Measures 4–6. Turn about and join left hands in centre and dance back to place with three 1-2-3-4 steps.

Measures 7–8. Clasp partner's both hands and dance once around in place. Two 1-2-3-4 steps.

Measures 9–14. All lead once around to place, gentlemen's left arms touching. Six 1-2-3-4 steps.

Measures 15–16. Turn hands over. Two 1-2-3-4 steps and salute.

IRISH FOUR HAND JIG.

OSTGOTAPOLSKA.

Formation. Eight couples in a set, two couples on each side facing centre. Four head couples and four side couples. (See Fig. 7, page 11.)

FIGURE 1. Gentlemen of head couples on right side of set, ladies of head couples on left side of set, stand behind partners with hands on partner's shoulders.

Measures 1–4. Bending heads alternately left and right play peek-a-boo with opposite for twelve counts.

Measures 5–6. Same dancers clap hands and with six running steps pass partners on left and advance to meet opposite in centre.

Measures 7–8. Join hands with opposite and turn with two Ostgota steps.

Measures 9–10. Drop hands, take own partner's both hands and turn with two Ostgota steps.

Measures 1–10. Other ladies and gentlemen of same couples repeat.

Measures 11–20. Side couples dance as described above, and repeat.

FIGURE 2. Gentlemen of couples on right of set and ladies of couples on left of set stand behind partners.

Measures 1–2. Dance six sliding steps to right, stamping on the first step.

Measures 3–4. Repeat to the left.

Measures 5–6. Clap hands and run six steps forward to meet opposite in centre of set.

Measures 7–8. Turn opposites two Ostgota steps.

Measures 9–10. Turn own partners with two Ostgota steps.

Measures 1–10. Other ladies and gentlemen of same couples repeat.

Measures 11–20. Side couples dance as described above, and repeat.

FIGURE 3. Gentlemen of head couples stamp left foot forward and kneel on right knee, right hand above head and holding ladies' left hand.

Measures 1–4. Ladies run once around partners with twelve running steps, starting towards front and describing a large circle.

Measures 5–6. Ladies run six steps across set, passing opposite lady on her right side.

Measures 7–8. Ladies run once around the gentleman of the opposite side, taking his right hand in her left.

Measures 9–10. All stand and turn partners in place with two Ostgota steps.

Measures 1–10. Repeat, ladies returning to their own partners.

Measures 11–20. Side couples repeat figure as described above, and repeat.

FIGURE 4. Grand chain.

Measures 1–10. Give right hands to partner and with thirty running steps, dance grand right and left around circle to place. Finish facing partners.

OSTGOTAPOLSKA (continued).

FIGURE 5. Cross over.

Measures 1–2. Head couples join inside hands, face towards each other and dance to opposite side of set with six sliding steps. Stamp on first step. Couples on left of set separate to allow couples on right of set to pass between them.

Measures 3–4. Side couples dance same across their side of set.

Measures 5–6. Head couples repeat, returning to place.

Measures 7–8. Side couples repeat, returning to place.

Measures 9–10. All turn partners two Ostgota steps. Finish in double circle, ladies on inside of set, facing outwards, hands joined; gentlemen standing close to partners, facing them.

FIGURE 6. Double circle.

Measures 11–20. All slide, ladies beginning right, gentlemen left, once around the circle to place.

Measures 11–20. Repeat Cross over as described in measures 1–10 of this figure.

Measures 1–10. Gentleman places hands on partner's hip. Lady places hands on gentleman's shoulder and all dance "Hambo" about the room.

FIG. 7. Two couples each side facing centre.

OSTGOTAPOLSKA.

GAMMAL POLKA.

Formation. Set of four couples, one couple standing on each of four corners of set, and all facing around set in same direction, ladies on the outside.

FIGURE 1. On sides of square.

Measures 1–16. With three polka steps on each side turning in place on fourth step, polka around four sides of set to place. Begin with outside foot. On last polka step, couples arrange themselves standing on corner of set and facing diagonally in toward the centre, and join left hands.

FIGURE 2. Facing diagonally to centre.

Measure 17. Gentleman starts right. Lady starts left. Polka step, lady crossing in front, gentleman in rear.

Measure 18. Polka step crossing back to place, lady in front, gentleman in rear.

Measure 19. Polka step crossing again, lady passing under gentleman's left arm to rear.

Measure 20. Lady curtseys, gentleman bows.

Measures 21–24. Repeat 17–20. This time the gentleman crosses in front.

Measures 25–28. Repeat 17–20.

Measures 29–23. Repeat 21–24.

FIGURE 3. On sides of square.

Measures 33–34. Two polka steps forward, lady turning in towards gentleman, and under his arm.

Measures 35–36. In waltz position take two polka steps forward, turning with partner.

Measures 37–40. Repeat 33–36 on second side of square.

Measures 33–40. Repeat on third and fourth side of square, and finish, partners facing on corners of set, ladies on the outside facing in.

FIGURE 4. On corner of set.

Measure 41. All start right foot, polka step to right side.

Measure 42. Point heel of left foot towards partner, and then toe of same foot behind right heel.

Measure 43. Repeat polka, starting left foot and turning to right, changing places with partner.

Measure 44. Point right toe to side and in back of left heel.

Measures 45–48. Repeat 42–44, returning to own place.

FIGURE 5.

Measure 41. Polka step forward, taking one half turn. Waltz position, gentleman starts left, lady starts right.

Measure 42. Gentleman points right toe at side and behind his left foot. Lady points left toe at side and behind her right foot.

Measures 43–48. Continue on for one side of square with same polka and point.

GAMMAL POLKA (continued).

Measures 1–4. In same waltz position, dance four polka steps, turning on second side of square.

Measures 5–12. Repeat measures 41–48. Polka step and point on third side of square.

Measures 13–15. Still in waltz position, dance three polka steps on last side of square.

Measure 16. Gentleman bow, and lady curtsey to partner.

GAMMAL POLKA (continued).

GAMMAL POLKA (continued).

IRISH SIX HAND REEL.

Formation. In set of six, two gentlemen and four ladies; one gentleman and two ladies on each side of set facing in towards the centre. Gentleman takes both ladies by the hands, elbows bent. All arms hang at sides unless otherwise indicated.

Step " Seven." 1. Spring and land lightly on both feet, right foot in advance.
2. Step right foot to side on ball of foot.
3. Step left foot across behind right.
4. Step right to right side.
5. Step left foot across behind right.
6 and 7. Repeat 4 and 5.

1-2-3-4 Step. 1–2. Hop on left foot and at same time step forward with right.
4. Bring left foot up to right. Left toe at heel of right foot.
5. Step forward. Right.

Short three. Swing left foot behind right and rest weight on it, and raise right foot (1). Change weight to right foot and raise left (2). Change weight to left foot and raise right foot (3).

FIGURE 1. Advance and retire.

Measures 1–2. Both lines advance to meet opposite with two 1-2-3-4 steps.
Measures 3–4. Retire, two 1-2-3-4 steps.
Measures 5–6. Advance, two 1-2-3-4 steps.
Measures 7–8. Retire, forming circle; ladies take hands at ends of set, two 1-2-3-4 steps.

FIGURE 2. Ring.

Measures 9–14. Dance in a ring, all hands joined to right six 1-2-3-4 steps.
Measures 15–16. Dance two " Short Threes " in place.
Measures 1–6. Dance back to left six 1-2-3-4 steps.
Measures 7–8. Two " Short Threes " ends separating, and all resuming original places in set.

FIGURE 3. Advance two.

Measures 9–10. Each gentleman crosses hands with lady on his right, dances one " seven step " across to opposite side of set with her. At same time lady on left of gentleman dances one " seven step " to opposite end of her side of set.
Measures 11–12. All dance two " short threes " in place.
Measures 13–14. All return to places with " seven step."
Measures 15–16. All dance in place two " short threes."
Measures 1–4. Each gentleman crosses hands with lady on left and repeats as in 9-12.
Measures 5–8. Return to place as in 13–16.

IRISH SIX HAND REEL (continued).

FIGURE 4. Reel. Link arms.

Measures 9–10. Each gentleman links right arm with lady on right and turns her with two 1-2-3-4 steps.

Measures 11–12. Gentleman quickly changes to lady on left and links left arm and turns with her with two 1-2-3-4 steps.

Measures 13–14. Repeat with lady on right.

Measures 15–16. Repeat with lady on left.

FIGURE 5. Side step to centre.

Measures 1–2. Lady on right moving to left and in front of gentleman, lady on left moving right and in rear of gentleman, dance across to opposite end of their side of set in one "seven step." At same time gentleman dances two "short threes" in place, turning right shoulder to opposite side of set.

Measures 3–4. Ladies dance two "short threes" in place. Gentlemen dance seven steps to opposite side of set, exchanging places.

Measures 5–6. Repeat as in 1–2, ladies returning to own places.

Measures 7–8. Repeat as in 3–4, gentlemen returning to own places.

Repeat all figures.

FINISH.

Measures 1–4. All give right hands in centre. Dance four 1-2-3-4 steps around in circle.

Measures 5–8. Each side of set join hands in small ring and dance four 1-2-3-4 steps by themselves, moving to the left.

Measures 9–12. All give left hands in centre. Dance four 1-2-3-4 steps around in circle.

Measures 13–16. Each side of set join hands in small ring and dance four 1-2-3-4 steps by themselves, moving to the right and finishing in their original places in the set.

IRISH SIX HAND REEL.

SAILOR'S HORNPIPE.

Formation. In rows.

Entrance. Run to front, bow, step back, and stand in preparation, arms folded and held well forward and shoulder high.

First Step. — Polka in Circle.

Measures 1–7. Seven polka steps moving in circle.

Measure 8. Three stamps in place, facing front ready for next step. The polka step is executed as follows.

Measure 1. Count 1. Step on right foot. Count 2. Bring up left foot so that side of foot touches heel of right foot. Count 3. Leap forward on right foot. Count 4. Pause. Repeat, starting left. This step is danced with very short steps, on the toes and with as much spring as possible. The step will be lighter if on count 1 the step on the right foot is immediately preceded by a hop on the left, in which case the count will be "and one, two, three."

Second Step. — Spy Glass.

Measure 9. Count 1. Left hand raised to forehead as if shading eyes, right hand on hip, elbow pointed out at side. Lean diagonally forward, bend right knee, slide right foot forward. Count 2. Bring up rear foot to right. Count 3. Slide right foot forward as in first count. Count 4. Hold position of arm and right leg, lifting left leg behind.

Measure 10. Count 1. Hop on right foot. Count 2. Hop on right foot. Count 3. Hop on right foot. Count 4. Hold.

Measures 11–16. Repeat all of second step as described in measures 9–10 to left, right and left.

Third Step. — Kick Step. Moving backward, hands on hips.

Measure 1. Count 1. Hop backward on left foot, at the same time raising right knee high and kick diagonally forward. Count 2. Repeat hop and kick on same foot. Count 3–4. Repeat 1 and 2, hopping backward on right and kicking left.

Measures 2–8. Repeat alternately left and right.

Fourth Step. — Rocking Step.

Measure 9. Count 1. Lock fingers, palms down. Swing right foot across in front of left so that the toe of the left is at the arch of the right, raise the left heel, slightly bend knees, and rock weight to right foot. Count 2. Raise right heel, rock weight to left foot. Count 3. Rock weight to right. Count 4. Swing left foot forward.

Measures 10–16. Repeat alternately left and right.

SAILOR'S HORNPIPE (continued).

FIFTH STEP. — Pulling Ropes (backward and forward).

Measure 1. Count 1. Step back on left foot, lean body forward, and both arms forward as if grasping a rope. Count 2. Draw right foot back to left, straighten trunk, pulling back with arms. Counts 3–4. Repeat.

Measures 2–4. Continue.

Measure 5. Counts 1–2–3–4. Raise hands chest high, right over left as if grasping a vertical rope. Run forward on heels eight steps, at the same time pulling rope down hand over hand.

Measures 6–8. Continue.

SIXTH STEP.

Measure 9. Count 1. Hands on hips. Jump to stride position. Count 2. Jump to feet across each other, right foot in front. Count 3. Touch right foot to right side. Count 4. Extend right foot forward.

Measure 10. Counts 1–2–3–4. Same left.

Measures 11–16. Repeat alternately right and left.

SEVENTH STEP.

Measure 1. Rolling — moving backward, arms folded shoulder high. Cross polka backward. Counts 1–2–3–4. Polka step toward left side, beginning by crossing right foot behind left, body leaning toward right.

Measure 2. Counts 1–2–3–4. Polka step toward right side, body rolling toward left.

Measures 3–8. Repeat alternately left and right.

EIGHTH STEP.—Trouser Hitch.

Exit Step. Moving forward in circle and then out. Right hand at waist line in front, left hand at waist line behind as if hitching up trousers.

Measure 1. Count 1. Lean forward and slide on right foot. Count 2. Hop on right, lifting left leg high behind. Count 3–4. Change arms and repeat step to left. Repeat to end of strain alternately left and right, or until out of room.

SAILOR'S HORNPIPE.

SWEDISH SCHOTTISCHE.

Formation. In couples, gentleman's right hand around lady's waist, left hand on own hip; lady's left hand on gentleman's shoulder, right hand on own hip; gentleman start left, lady start right.

Measures 1–4. Eight walking steps, clicking heel on floor before each step.

Measures 5–8. Eight hop waltz steps forward.

Measures 9–10. Two schottische steps forward, lady turning under gentleman's arm.

Measures 11–12. Four hop waltz steps, turning in waltz position.

Measures 13–16. Repeat measures 9–12.

Measures 17–18. Gentleman's arms folded, lady's hands on hips, two schottische steps forward; lady dancing backward and facing gentleman.

Measures 19–20. Waltz position — four hop waltz steps turning.

Measures 21–24. Repeat measures 19–20.

Measures 25–26. Gentleman two schottische steps in place; lady turning to left around man with two schottische steps.

Measures 27–28. Side by side, in original position, four hop waltz steps forward.

Measures 29–32. Repeat measures 25–28.

Measures 1–12. Arms crossed in back and hands joined with partner's, start to left with left foot, three hop waltz steps to left and point right heel forward towards left.

Measures 3–4. Repeat, starting right and moving right.

Measures 5–8. Repeat measures 1–4.

Measures 9–10. Gentleman kneels on right knee, lady starting in front, takes two schottische steps around man.

Measures 11–12. Both dance four hop waltz steps forward in original position.

Measures 13–16. Repeat measures 9–12.

Measures 17–18. Lady faces gentleman and crosses in front of him again, two schottische steps.

Measures 19–20. Four hop waltz steps, turning in waltz position.

Measures 21–32. Repeat measures 17–20; on last measure gentleman lifts lady high in the air and sets her down again.

Note: Hop Waltz. Step right, hop right, step left, hop left.

SWEDISH SCHOTTISCHE.

SWEDISH SCHOTTISCHE (continued).

VIRGINIA REEL.

Formation. Sets of eight or more couples in two lines about four feet apart. Partners opposite, all facing centre. (No. 1 in one line, No. 2 in other line.)

Step. Skip-step or spring-step.

Note: Nos. 1 of head couple and 2 of foot couple lead in each figure. Nos. 2 of head couple and 1 of foot couple repeat the figure.

Figure 1. Balance corners. Forward to centre, bow to partner and backward to position.

Figure 2. Forward to centre, join right hands and turn. Backward to position.

Figure 3. Repeat figure, joining left hands.

Figure 4. Repeat figure, joining both hands.

Figure 5. Forward to centre, pass back to back, right shoulders first, backward to position.

Figure 6. Repeat figure, passing with left shoulders first.

Figure 7. Head couple join both hands, arms extended, slide-step (slide, close) to foot and back to head of set.

Figure 8. Head couple hook right arms (or join right hands) and turn one and one half times to place. Give left hand to neighbor on opposite side and turn once around. Right arm to partner and turn once around. Continue down the line, turning partner and neighbor alternately to the foot of set. Turn partner one and one half times around and take position for slide-step.

Figure 9. Slide-step to head of set, to foot of set and back to head.

Figure 10. Head couple drop hands and all face forward. Head couple lead off turning towards foot of set on outside of set. Others follow, all clapping. At foot, head couple join hands and continue to position at head of line. Face each other, join both hands and form arch by raising both arms. Other couples follow, taking their own places in line and forming arch. Last couple pass through arch to head of set. All drop hands and take proper distance. Repeat the dance till all couples are in their original position.

VIRGINIA REEL.

VIRGINIA REEL (continued).

FRYKDALS POLSKA.

Formation. In sets of four couples, two couples on each side of set facing centre. Number couples, 1 and 2 in left hand line, and 3 and 4 in right hand line.

Step. Frykdals step. Stamp left foot to side, bring right foot up to left, hop on right and raise left at side. The step is always begun with the left foot.

FIGURE 1.

Measures 1–4. Couples 1 and 2 join hands in small ring; couples 3 and 4 the same, and all dance four Frykdals steps moving left.

Measures 5–8. Continue to left with four Frykdals steps, but change grasp. Gentleman takes thumb grasp with right hand in centre, lady places right hand on gentleman's wrist. All place left hand on shoulder of one in front.

Measures 9–16. Gentleman places both hands at partner's waist, lady places both hands on partner's shoulders and all dance eight Frykdals steps turning to place. The set is now in its original position, all facing the centre.

FIGURE 2.

Measures 1–2. Lady runs six steps to opposite gentleman, giving right hand to opposite lady in passing.

Measures 3–4. Gentleman takes lady's left hand in his left, places his right arm about her waist and turns her around to the right with six running steps.

Measures 5–8. Gentleman stands behind lady with both hands at her waist, she with both hands on her hips, and all do four Bleeking steps in place. Thus: man springs and points left heel forward and bends slightly towards his partner to the right; lady springs and points right heel forward and bends slightly to right, turning towards her partner. All spring and change feet, bending slightly to opposite side.

Measures 9–10. Ladies return to own partner with six running steps.

Measures 11–12. Turn with partner as described before in measures 3–4.

Measures 13–16. Gentleman places both hands at lady's waist, lady places hands on gentleman's shoulders and couples turn to place with four Frykdals steps.

FIGURE 3.

Measures 1–2. Both couples of each line join hands. All run forward six steps to meet opposite line, and both ends of lines join hands.

Measures 3–4. All run six steps backward and pull out into a circle.

Measures 5–6. All run six steps forward; this time forming in two lines at right angles to first two lines.

Measures 7–8. All run six steps backward, pulling out into circle.

FRYKDALS POLSKA. (continued).

Measures 9–10. All run six steps forward, forming lines as in measures 1–2 of this figure.

Measures 11–12. All run six steps backward, pulling out into circle again.

Measures 13–16. Turn partners to place with four Frykdals steps.

FIGURE 4.

Measures 1–8. Ladies run forward to centre of set and join right hands, thumb grasp, holding partners' right hand in their left. With twenty-four running steps, the whole set wheels in a clock-wise direction.

Measures 9–16. Ladies drop grasp, each couple wheels about and gentlemen take thumb grasp with left hands. With twenty-four running steps the whole set wheels back again.

Measures 1–8. Turn partners to original place with eight Frykdals steps.

Measures 9–16. All wait in place.

FIGURE 5.

Measures 1–8. Couples 3 and 4 face front and form arch by holding inside joined hands high. Couples 1 and 2 join hands in string, and lady of couple 1 runs forward leading the string through the arch formed by couples 3 and 4. While the string is passing through the arch the couples holding the arch dance quick kicking-steps in place, flinging the foot forward on each step. As the man of couple number 2 passes through arch held by couple number 3, he takes the right hand of the lady of couple number 3 and pulls the couple after him; they join the string and in the same way the man of couple number 3 takes right hand of lady in couple number 4, and pulls that couple along with string. As couples number 1 and 2 reach their places, they spring into place facing front and hold the arch, dancing kicking-steps in place. Couples number 3 and 4 run on through arch held by number 1 and 2, and continue to their places. Couple number 3 swings into place and holds arch. Number 4 passes through arch, swings into place and all dance kicking-steps in place until the end of eight measures.

Measures 9–16. All turn partners in place with eight Frykdals steps.

FIGURE 6.

Measures 1–3. Couples 1 and 2 join hands in ring, and couples 3 and 4 join hands in ring, all dance four Frykdals steps, swinging to left in circle. On fourth step, couples 1 and 3 change over into the opposite circle.

Measures 5–8. Both circles continue on to left with four Frykdals steps; on fourth step, couples 2 and 4 change over to opposite circles.

Measures 9–16. Repeat measures 1–8.

Measures 1–8. Turn partners in place eight Frykdals steps.

FRYKDALS POLSKA.

DALDANS.

Formation. In sets. Couples standing one behind the other and facing front. As many couples as will. Gentleman unless otherwise directed folds arms on chest. Lady places hands on hips.

FIGURE 1.

Measures 1–8 and repeat. Sixteen Dal steps around in circle to right and to place. Couples begin with right foot and follow leaders. Gentleman's arms folded across chest. Lady's left hand on gentleman's shoulder, right hand on hip.

FIGURE 2.

Measures 9–10. All face towards partners, join both hands and dance two Dal steps in place.

Measures 11–12. Turn pancake. Turn in place, lady turning right under her right arm, man turning left under his left arm, with six running steps. Both hands joined.

Measures 13–16. Repeat measures 9–12.

FIGURE 3.

Measures 17–18. Cross to opposite side of set with six running steps.

Measure 19. Face in towards centre, and kick three steps in place.

Measure 20. Salute. Jump and land on both feet in stride position, arms thrust out at side; on count three jump, bringing feet together, hands on hips.

Measures 21–24. Repeat measures 17–20, returning to own side of set.

Measures 17–24. Repeat all.

FIGURE 4.

Measures 25–32. All dance eight Dal steps towards partners, beginning with right foot.

Measures 25–32. Join hands with partner and dance eight Bleeking steps in place. Place right foot forward resting on heels and change feet by springing off the floor and bending knee high.

FIGURE 5.

Measures 1–8. Lady dances eight waltz steps, turning to right in place. Gentleman dances eight Dal steps in circle around lady from left to right, clapping hands once on each step.

FIGURE 6.

Measures 1–2. Partners face each other and join hands. Turn pancake as in Figure 2, but this time quickly, using only three steps.

Measure 3. Lady kneels on right knee.

Measure 4. Gentleman steps forward with left, kicks right foot over lady's head to left and turns around to left pivoting on left foot, steps on right foot pivoting to left and springs to original position, landing feet together.

Measures 5–8. Repeat measures 1–4.

Measures 9–12. Repeat measures 1–4.

Measures 13–16. Repeat measures 1–4.

FIGURE 7.

Measures 17–18. Lady dances diagonally forward away from partner with step and balance right and left.

Measure 19. Kick in place three times.

Measure 20. Salute as in Figure 3, measure 20.

Measures 21–24. Repeat measures 17–20.

Measures 17–24. Eight waltz steps turning to right, moving back to place opposite partner.

FIGURE 8.

Measures 25–26. Partners face, and gentleman beginning with left foot, lady with right, step forward with knee bent and body leaning forward and hop. Same with other foot.

Measure 27. Spring away from partner, gentleman turning to left and landing on left foot and hop on same, lady to right landing on right foot and hop on same.

Measure 28. Jump and turn in same direction and land feet together in original places.

Measures 29–32. Repeat measures 25–28.

Measures 25–32. Repeat all.

FIGURE 9.

Measures 1–4. All run to centre, hook right arms and turn right with twelve running steps.

Measures 5–8. Change to left arms and turn to left with twelve running steps.

FIGURE 10.

Measures 1–2. Take position as at the beginning of dance. All dance two Dal steps in place beginning with left foot.

Measures 3–4. Gentleman places both hands at partner's waist. Lady places hands on partner's shoulders. Gentleman stamps left foot, lifts lady up and places her on his left. Lady assists by springing from the floor.

Measures 5–8. Repeat, this time gentleman places lady on his right.

Measures 9–16. Repeat measures 1–8 of this figure.

DALDANS (continued).

Figure 11.

Measures 17–24. Gentleman dances eight Dal steps, diagonally forward away from partner, stamping foot and swinging arms alternately across in front and behind.

Measures 17–24. Gentleman dances back to position opposite partner with eight saluting steps, thrusting thumbs out at sides when in stride position and placing hands on hips when feet are together.

Figure 12.

Measure 25. Partners cross hands. Lady springs two steps across in front of partner, landing on his left, feet together. Gentleman assists by pulling her.

Measure 26. Gentleman springs to left of lady in same way.

Measure 27. Lady springs to left of gentleman.

Measure 28. Wait in place.

Measures 29–32. Repeat above, this time each springs to right of partner.

Figure 13.

Measures 25–32. Gentleman stands behind lady with both hands at her waist. Lady places both hands on hips. Both dance eight Dal steps in place. Gentleman begins right, lady left, and both turn towards partner on each step.

Figure 14.

Measures 1–8. Gentleman faces partner and puts both hands at her waist. Lady places both hands on partner's shoulders. All dance Hambo around the room. Gentleman begins left, steps left foot backward, hops on left, turns to right and steps right foot to side. Lady starts right, steps right foot forward, hops on right, turns to right and steps left foot to side.

DALDANS.

DALDANS (continued).

SPRING DANCE.

Formation. In couples, moving about room, counter clock-wise.

Measures 1–16. Man takes lady's left hand in his right and leads her forward with running steps, three to each measure, both beginning with right foot.

Measures 1–8. Man stamps on first beat of measure 1, and then dances change-steps in place (step, together step,) to end of measure 8. Lady dances under man's right arm with running step, turning first to outside then to inside and to outside again. The man then swings his arm down, and with a stamp springs forward in front of his partner.

Measures 9–16. Man leads forward and lady follows, both using twelve step hops.

Measures 1–8. Man stamps forward with right foot and turns to right, at the same time moving forward; in this way, step right, step left, and snap heels together completing the turn. Continue turning once to each measure. Lady follows man and dances same step, but less vigorously.

Measures 9–16. "Coketering." The man stamps his right foot and faces lady. Both move to man's left with six side running steps, three steps to a measure, the man placing his right foot and the lady her left behind each time. Repeat six running steps, moving to man's right. Repeat, moving to man's left and right. On the last count the man makes a dash for the lady who slips under his right arm, circles around him to her right and follows him again.

Measures 1–16.
1–16.
1–16. } Repeat all of the dance as described.

Measures 1–8. On last count of coketering the lady gives her right hand to gentleman, who takes it in his right. He swings her about, taking her left hand in his left and turns her with running steps, first to right, then to left. In turning to right the lady leans against his left arm, and turning to left she is against his right arm.

Measures 9–16. The man takes lady's hands in his right and holds them above her head. He dances change-steps in place, and she turns under his arm, first to right with twelve running steps and then to left.

Measures 1–8. Repeat "Coketering."

Measures 9–16. "Roll Partner." Man hooks his left arm in lady's right and revolves her around him, changing arms from his left in her right to his right in her left. Man dances change-steps in place, lady uses running steps.

SPRING DANCE.

HALLING.

Halling is usually done by one man at a time, but may be done by a number moving in a single circle.

Measures 1–8. With clenched fists held at sides about shoulder high, strut forward sixteen steps, beginning with right foot.

Measures 9–16. Step-hop eight times forward, and eight times backward, raising knee of free foot slightly on each hop.

Measures 17–24. Two strutting steps forward, one step-hop, raising heel of free foot to knee of other foot, and continue throughout measures.

Measures 25–32. Change step and hop once to each measure throughout measures. Step right foot forward, bring left up, right forward again. Hop on right and raise left knee. Repeat left and right to end of measures.

Measures 32–40. Step-hop, and on every third hop raise heel of free foot to side and strike it with hand of same side. This brings the striking alternately left and right.

Measures 1–8. Strut forward and on the last beat of every other measure jump from floor and strike both heels with hands.

Measures 9–10. Step-hop forward four times.

Measures 11–12. Step right foot forward. Hop right, raise left heel behind and strike it with right hand. Hop right and strike left heel with left hand, hop right, raise left heel in front and strike it with right hand.

Measures 13–14. Step-hop four times forward, beginning with left foot.

Measures 15–16. Repeat measures 11–12, hopping on left foot and striking right heel.

Measures 17–24. Strut forward, on every third step kick first the left elbow with the left toes, and alternate right and left to end of measures. This must be done by bending the knee sharply, foot as far to outside as possible, and bringing elbow down by bending at waist.

Measures 25–32. Stand with hands fastened behind neck, elbows out at sides. Bend knees as deeply as possible, and strike right elbow to ground. Repeat striking left elbow to ground. Repeat alternately eight times in all.

Measures 32–40. With arms swinging loosely at sides, turn to right, progressing around in circle with following step: Step right, step left, step right, hop right and kick left in front. Same beginning left. The dance is usually finished with the Halling Kast, which is a high kick originally done in an effort to kick the middle beam in the old Norwegian houses, but now done to kick the gentleman's hat, which is held high by a lady standing on a chair.

HALLING.

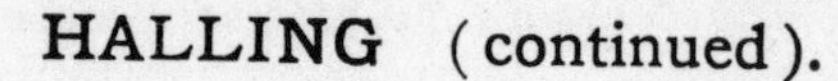

HALLING (continued).

MAY-POLE DANCE.

Formation. Double circle (See Fig. 1, page 8) around May-pole. All face forward around circle, inside hands joined and held high, outside hands holding skirts. Number couples off in threes.

Measures 1–8. Partners move around circle twelve skip-steps. Form large circle, inside partner turning in place, outside moving by her side. Finish facing centre, all hands joined in one large circle.

Measures 9–10. Forward four skip-steps, heads well up.

Measures 11–12. Backward four skip-steps.

Measures 13–16. Repeat forward and backward.

Measures 17–24. Join right hands with partner and turn in places sixteen skip-steps. Hold skirts with left hand. Finish in double circle, partners facing each other.

Measures 1–2. Hold skirts with both hands and polka to right side, point left foot diagonally forward, and touch left toe behind right heel.

Measures 3–4. Repeat left, pointing right toe forward and in back.

Measures 5–8. Repeat right and left.

Measures 9–16. Join right hands with partner and turn with eight polka steps. Finish in single circle.

Measures 17–24. All join hands and skip four steps to centre and four back to place, and repeat.

Measures 1–2. Couples number 1; skip four steps to centre with partner and each take a ribbon in her right hand.

Measures 3–4. Return to place with four skip-steps.

Measures 5–8. Couples number 2 the same.

Measures 9–12. Couples number 3 the same.

Measures 13–16. All face partners and wait in place.

Measures 17–24. Chain (grand right and left) around pole sixteen skip-steps. Start passing with right shoulders together. Hold skirts with left hand, ribbon in right hand.

Measures 1–8. All forward four skip-steps and drop ribbons. Backward four skip-steps to position, all joining hands. Repeat step forward and backward.

Measures 9–24. All skip eight steps to left, eight steps to right and continue; leader leading circle away from the May-pole.

MAY-POLE DANCE.

BLUFF KING HAL.

MAY-POLE DANCE (continued).

33909